Gladys Aylward

Are you going to stop?

The true story of Gladys Aylward
and her orphanage

Catherine Mackenzie
Illustrated by Rita Ammassari

There was once a little lady who lived in the big city of London. Her name was Gladys Aylward. She worked in a posh house as a parlour maid, fetching and carrying, serving food, cleaning clothes and running messages.

Gladys was quite different from the tall elegant ladies who visited the house; she was small, with dark eyes and dark hair. Sometimes she wished she'd been born tall, with blonde hair and blue eyes instead, but that didn't stop Gladys. She trusted in God and knew that he had made her this way.

Gladys was quite different from the tall elegant ladies who visited the house; she was small, with dark eyes and dark hair.

Ever since she'd been a teenager, Gladys had wanted to go abroad as a missionary. But her family was poor and couldn't afford to give her the money for her ticket. She was from a working class background and hadn't spent much time in school.

The people who ran the missions thought, 'That girl will never be able to learn the language. She's not clever enough.' But that didn't stop Gladys hoping and planning. Gladys trusted in God and knew that his plans were the best.

Gladys trusted in God and knew that his plans were the best.

'How will I get to China?' Gladys wondered. 'I'm not rich enough. I'm not clever enough. I wonder if I'll ever get to work as a missionary?' But Gladys didn't stop. She saved every penny she could.

Month after month, year after year, Gladys hoped and prayed and saved. One way or another, Gladys was going to China. She trusted in God and knew that nothing stopped him.

Gladys didn't stop. She saved every penny she could.

After four years of hard saving, when Gladys was thirty years old, a letter arrived for her from China. An elderly lady missionary needed an assistant. Jeannie Lawson heard that Gladys wanted to serve God in China, so she asked her to come and help her carry on her missionary work.

Jeannie couldn't help Gladys with the cost of her tickets, but that didn't stop Gladys. She trusted in God and went to buy the cheapest ticket she could afford. With her tickets, her Bible and her passport, Gladys had all she needed to travel to China.

Gladys had all she needed to travel to China.

It was a long and dangerous journey by rail through Europe and on to Siberia. Eventually, she arrived at the Chinese city of Yangchen. As she looked around the bustling city, she received an answer to a question she'd been asking all her life. 'I often wondered,' Gladys thought, 'why God made me small and dark instead of tall and blonde. Now I know.' Every single Chinese person as far as the eye could see was small and dark. There wasn't a single blonde-haired blue-eyed person for miles.

'I often wondered,' Gladys thought, 'why God made me small and dark instead of tall and blonde. Now I know.'

It took a while for Gladys to settle into her work. The people of the Shansi province didn't trust foreigners. However, Jeannie put Gladys to work in turning their home into an inn for the mule drivers who visited the city. But Gladys didn't know the language. How could she get the mule drivers to come to their inn?

Gladys had an idea. She ran out into the street and grabbed hold of a mule. Then she dragged the mule train into the courtyard. The mule drivers had to follow. Eventually the clean beds, good food and excellent stories made the Inn of Sixth Happiness a popular place to stay.

Gladys had an idea. She ran out into the street and grabbed hold of a mule.

Gladys did her best to learn the local language and soon she was able to tell stories to the mule drivers by herself. Gladys was able to talk to the mule drivers as they ate their meals. She was able to stop and talk to the children who came to see what all the fuss was about. She loved to tell the Chinese people the good news about Jesus Christ.

The mission organisations had been wrong about Gladys. She may not have had a great education – but Gladys was a great storyteller. She just kept on going whatever faced her.

Gladys was able to talk to the mule drivers as they ate their meals.

After Jeannie's death, Gladys carried on with the work. She started visiting other villages in order to help the women and children there. Gladys started an orphanage and even adopted some children herself. One little girl was being sold at the side of the road, so Gladys bought her. She cost nine-pence and so that was what Gladys called her.

One day Nine-pence found a little boy on the side of the road. 'Can we keep him, Mother?' she asked. 'I'll eat less so that he can stay,' she said. Gladys agreed and the little boy was named 'Less'. Gladys' orphanage grew. Soon she had 100 children.

Gladys started an orphanage and even adopted some children herself.

There came a time when the world was at war. Germany fought against the United Kingdom and other European countries. Japan fought against the United States and China. Gladys became a citizen of China at that time and even did some spying against the Japanese. Soon she had a price on her head and was warned by a Chinese General to escape while she still could. Gladys quickly gathered up all the children and fled from the city – just in time.

There were no lorries or carts to carry the children across the mountains. So they all had to walk through very difficult countryside, dodging Japanese troops as they went.

Gladys quickly gathered up all the children and fled from the city – just in time.

After many days Gladys and the children came face to face with the huge Yellow River. But there was no bridge to be seen or any boats. Gladys didn't know how they were going to get across. The Japanese troops weren't far away and their lives were in great danger. 'Why don't we cross it like Moses crossed the Red Sea?' a little boy asked.

'Because I'm not Moses,' Gladys grumbled.

'But God's still God,' the little boy replied.

Gladys and the children came face to face with the huge Yellow River.

Gladys had to admit it was true, when all of a sudden a boat arrived with Chinese soldiers on board. They quickly transported them across the river to safety. The 100 mile journey with 100 orphans was finally over.

Gladys continued to work for her Lord and Saviour, Jesus Christ. She helped to set up a church and shared the good news of Jesus in villages, in prisons and in hospitals.

The little lady from London could not be stopped, because she went forward in the strength of her unstoppable God.

The 100 mile journey with 100 orphans was finally over.

This book is dedicated to the memory of three missionaries:
Meg Byres, Annie Macangus and Dolina Mackenzie.
They never left for foreign mission fields, but their work and
influence for Christ's Kingdom has been far-reaching.

10 9 8 7 6 5 4 3 2 1
© Copyright 2013 Catherine Mackenzie
ISBN: 978-1-78191-161-7
Published by Christian Focus Publications,
Geanies House, Fearn, Tain, Ross-shire, IV20 1TW, Scotland, U.K.
www.christianfocus.com
Cover design by Daniel van Straaten
Printed in China
Other titles in this series:
Corrie ten Boom: Are all of the watches safe? 978-1-84550-109-9
Amy Carmichael: Can brown eyes be made blue? 978-1-84550-108-2
David Livingstone: Who is the bravest? 978-1-84550-384-0
John Calvin: What is the Truth? 978-1-84550-560-8
George Müller: Does money grow on trees? 978-1-84550-110-5
Helen Roseveare: What's in the parcel? 978-1-84550-383-3
Eric Liddell: Are you ready? 978-1-84550-790-9
Mary Slessor: What is it like? 978-1-84550-791-6
C. S. Lewis: Can you imagine? 978-1-78191-160-0